POLISH IMMIGRANTS

1890-1920

by Rosemary Wallner

Content Consultant:
John Radzilowski, Ph.D.
Editor of *Periphery: Journal of Polish Affairs*
Second vice-president of the Polish American Historical Association
Polish American Studies editorial board member
Past president of the Polish American Cultural Institute of Minnesota

Blue Earth Books

an imprint of Capstone Press
Mankato, Minnesota

Blue Earth Books are published by Capstone Press,
151 Good Counsel Drive, P.O. Box 669, Mankato, Minnesota 56002.
www.capstonepress.com

102009
5626R

Library of Congress Cataloging-in-Publication Data
Wallner, Rosemary, 1964–
   Polish immigrants, 1890–1920 / by Rosemary Wallner; content consultant, John Radzilowski.
      p. cm. — (Coming to America)
   Includes bibliographical references and index.
   Summary: Discusses the reasons Polish people left their homeland to come to America, the experiences the immigrants had in the new country, and the
contributions this cultural group made to American society. Includes sidebars and activities.
   ISBN-13: 978-0-7368-1208-5 (Reinforced Library Binding)
   ISBN-10: 0-7368-1208-3 (Reinforced Library Binding)

   1. Polish Americans—History—Juvenile literature. 2. Immigrants—United States—History—Juvenile literature. 3. Poland—Emigration and
immigration—History—Juvenile literature. 4. United States—Emigration and immigration—History—Juvenile literature. [1. Polish Americans—History.
2. Immigrants—History. 3. United States—Emigration and immigration—History. 4. Polish—Emigration and immigration—History.] I. Radzilowski,
John, 1965– II. Title III. Coming to America (Mankato, Minn.)
   E184.P7 W335 2003
   973'.049185—dc21
                                                                                          2001005867

Editorial credits
Editors: Kay M. Olson and Katy Kudela
Series Designer: Heather Kindseth
Book Designer: Jennifer Schonborn
Photo Researcher: Stacy Foster
Product Planning Editor: Karen Risch

Photo credits
Bettmann/CORBIS, cover, 10, 11, 14; Gregg Andersen, flag images
throughout; CORBIS, 4; Leonard de Selva/CORBIS, 6; Stock
Montage, Inc., 7; Library of Congress, 8, 20, 21; Capstone Press/Gary
Sundermeyer, 9, 25; Austrian Archives/CORBIS, 13; Hulton/Archive
Photos, 15, 29 (bottom); National Archives, 17; Underwood &
Underwood/CORBIS, 18; James L. Amos/CORBIS, 19; Sandy
Felsenthal/CORBIS, 22, 24; Kelly-Mooney Photography/CORBIS,
23; The Syrena Polish Folk Dance Ensemble, Milwaukee, WI/Photo
by James Panka, 26; Reuters NewsMedia Inc./CORBIS, 29 (top)

Contents

Chapter 1—Early Polish Immigrants 4

Chapter 2—Life in the Old Country 6

Chapter 3—The Trip Over 10

Chapter 4—Arriving in America 14

Chapter 5—Surviving in America 18

Chapter 6—Keeping Traditions 22

Features

Immigration Route Map 5

Make a Family Tree 27

Timeline 28

Famous Polish Americans 29

Words to Know 30

To Learn More 31

Places to Write and Visit 31

Internet Sites 32

Index 32

POLISH IMMIGRANTS 1890 TO 1920

EARLY POLISH IMMIGRANTS

Polish men often traveled to America alone. When they earned enough money, they sent for their wives and children.

D uring the 1600s, Poland was a powerful and wealthy country. Nobles made up 10 percent of Poland's population. Most of these nobles were poor, but they influenced political decisions. It was the nobles' duty to protect the country and its citizens.

By the 1650s, Poland suffered from political and military troubles. Government changes caused some people to leave Poland. A number of Polish immigrants traveled to America to fight in the Revolutionary War (1775–1783). During the early 1800s, some of Poland's poorer nobles also fled to America. In 1854, the first Polish community in America was established in Panna Maria, Texas.

Large-scale Polish immigration to the United States started in the 1870s. At first, Polish men came to America by themselves. They hoped to earn money and return home to buy land. Soon Polish men, women, and children were working many hours in factories and coal mines just to survive.

Several waves of Polish immigrants arrived in America during the late 1880s and 1900s. By 1880, about 500,000 Poles had come to America. That number increased to 1 million between 1881 and 1900. The largest group of Poles came to America between 1901 and 1920, when about 2 million Polish immigrants arrived.

Today, the largest numbers of Polish Americans live in cities such as Chicago, New York City, Detroit, Philadelphia, and Buffalo, New York. More than 9.3 million people in the United States today are Polish Americans.

Immigration Route

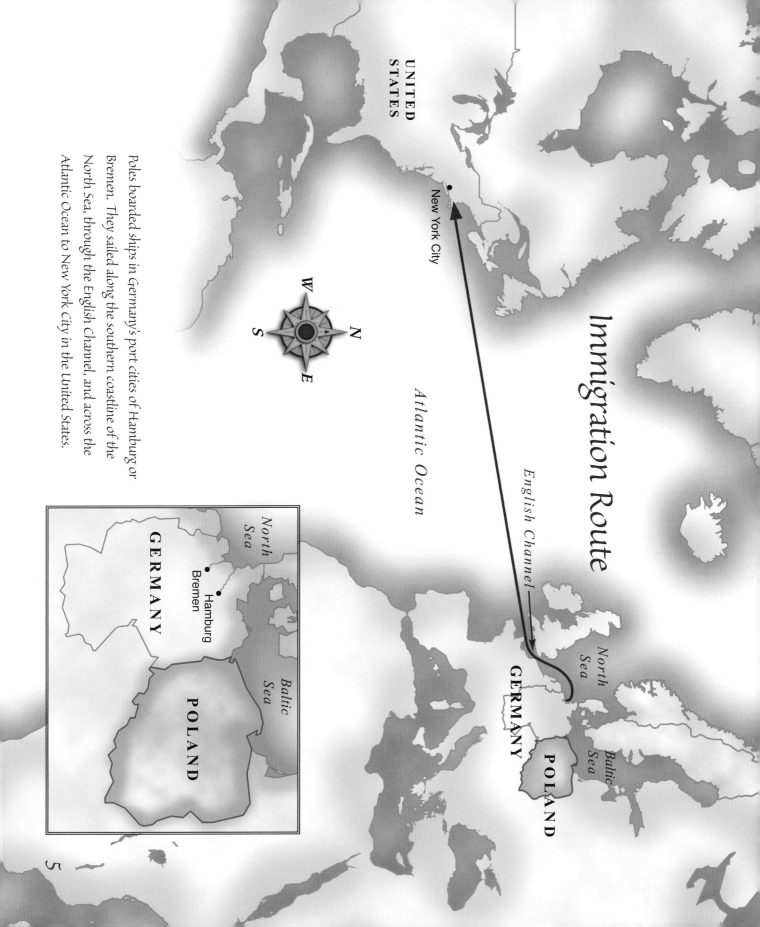

Poles boarded ships in Germany's port cities of Hamburg or Bremen. They sailed along the southern coastline of the North Sea, through the English Channel, and across the Atlantic Ocean to New York City in the United States.

UNITED STATES

New York City

Atlantic Ocean

English Channel

North Sea

GERMANY

POLAND

Baltic Sea

North Sea

GERMANY

Hamburg
Bremen

Baltic Sea

POLAND

N
W · E
S

5

LIFE IN THE OLD COUNTRY

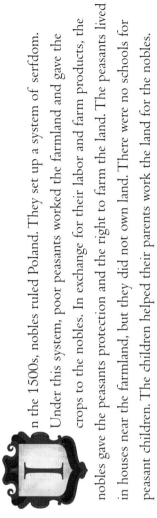

Polish nobles ruled Poland from the 1500s until the late 1700s. They owned much of the land, lived in fine castles, and wore fancy clothes.

I n the 1500s, nobles ruled Poland. They set up a system of serfdom. Under this system, poor peasants worked the farmland and gave the crops to the nobles. In exchange for their labor and farm products, the nobles gave the peasants protection and the right to farm the land. The peasants lived in houses near the farmland, but they did not own land. There were no schools for peasant children. The children helped their parents work the land for the nobles.

For 200 years the nobles ruled Poland. During the 1650s, Poland suffered from military and political troubles. The nobles began to fight among themselves. By the 1700s, the Polish army was weak. Poland had a weak central government that was unable to unite the country.

In 1772 and again in 1793, Russia, Prussia (later called Germany), and Austria invaded Poland. The rulers of these three countries wanted Poland's land for themselves. These countries knew that the Polish nobles and peasants did not have a strong army to defend their country. Russia, Prussia, and Austria each conquered a part of Poland. The Poles tried to resist, but no other nation would help them. A last invasion in 1795 erased Poland as a country.

From 1795 to 1917, Russia, Prussia, and Austria each ruled a part of Poland. The rulers of these countries created many new laws. In Prussian Poland, it was sometimes against the law to speak Polish.

Prussian officials built schools, but the children were taught mainly in German. In some regions, they continued to teach religion in Polish. In Russian Poland, there were very few schools. Galicia was the name for the part of Poland that Austria occupied. Galicia was a poor region that had its own government. In the late 1800s, this government was mostly Polish.

The nobles rebelled against these new rulers. They started secret schools where the teachers used the Polish language. If the foreign rulers found out about these schools, they arrested the teachers.

The majority of Polish peasants saw little difference between being ruled by Polish nobility or foreigners. The farmers were still poor and could not keep all of the crops for themselves. Peasant farmers still built their homes alongside the road. Their fields stretched out behind the homes.

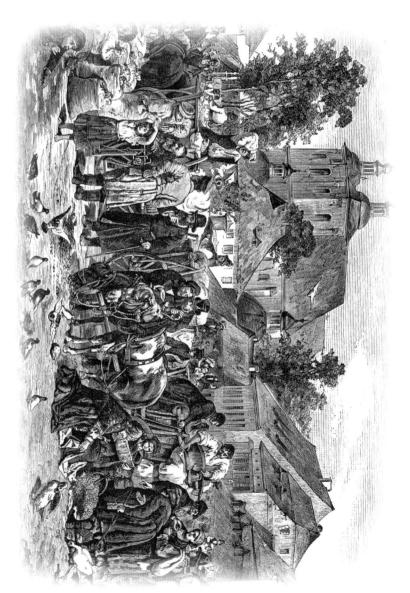

In the 1800s, most peasant farm families in Poland lived in small villages.

Family was very important to the Polish peasants. Grandparents, parents, and children often lived together in a single cottage. When a father was too old to work, he divided the land he farmed among his sons. He and his wife then would live with one of their sons and his family.

Polish parents loved their children, but they expected them to work hard. Children fed the cows, goats, pigs, and

7

" . . . What we do for amusement when I am a boy in Poland? We played only about the yard or the barn, for we work very hard and long hours on the farm. When we play it is mostly to play soldiers, always, and talk a great deal about war and battles for at that time where I live we are under Austrian rule, for Poland was partitioned to Austria, Russia, and Germany. It was partitioned three times and did not be free until 1918."

—Adam Laboda,
Pittsfield, Massachusetts, 1938

In the late 1800s, Polish peasants began to hear stories about free land in America. Many farmers began to leave Poland and immigrate to the United States.

other livestock. At age 10, boys and girls began helping their parents gather crops.

Hardworking peasants also had fun and kept their traditions. When a baby was christened, the whole village took time to celebrate the occasion. Most Poles were Roman Catholics, and they celebrated the church's holy days. At Easter, they decorated eggs with brightly colored dyes and fancy designs. This egg decorating, called pisanki, is still popular today.

By the late 1800s, the population in Prussian Poland, Russian Poland, and Galicia had grown larger. Farms became smaller each time a father divided the land he farmed between his sons. Sometimes the grown sons left the farm and looked for work in one of the large cities, such as Kraków or Warsaw.

Government officials found it difficult to manage the peasants. They did not want to deal with peasant labor and farm products. Instead, the government required the peasants to pay rent on their land.

Polish peasants were in need of cash for the first time. Under the old system, the peasants were able to grow, make, or trade for the things they needed.

★ Pisanki: Egg Decorating ★

Pisanki is the traditional Polish art of decorating eggs. To preserve an eggshell, prick a hole in each end of the egg with a safety pin. Insert a thin wire, scramble the yolk and white, and gently blow all of the insides out of the shell. When decorating your egg, you will need an adult's help to light the candle and melt the wax.

What You Need

egg (with insides removed)	candle and matches
vinegar	beeswax*
paper towels	dyes* (yellow, orange,
stylus* (a metal,	purple)
pen-shaped instrument)	spoon

facial tissues

clear, glossy varnish

waxed paper

*available in most craft stores

What You Do

1. Wipe the egg with a paper towel moistened in vinegar.
2. Ask an adult to heat the end of the stylus over a candle flame. Press the hot stylus into the beeswax.
3. Use the wax that sticks to the stylus to create a simple decoration on the egg.
4. Place the egg in the yellow dye for 10 minutes. Use the spoon to remove the egg and pat it dry with a paper towel. Let the egg air dry for 5 minutes.
5. Repeat step 3. Place the egg in the orange dye for 10 minutes. Pat dry and allow to air dry for 5 minutes.

6. Repeat step 3. Place the egg in the purple dye for 10 minutes. Pat dry and allow to air dry for 5 minutes.
7. When the egg is completely dry, ask an adult to hold the egg near the candle flame so that the wax melts and becomes shiny. Gently wipe off the wax with a facial tissue. Repeat until the entire egg is clean.
8. Varnish deepens the color and preserves the egg. Dip your index finger into the varnish and spread the varnish over the egg. Put on two coats of the varnish. Let the egg dry on a piece of waxed paper. Wipe your finger clean.

THE TRIP OVER

Polish women often traveled to America by themselves. Many married and unmarried Polish immigrants came to America. The men usually arrived first.

Most Poles who emigrated from their country had no special skills or education. They were mostly farmers who wanted a chance to own land and feed their families. Men usually traveled to America first. They planned to find a job and earn money. With the money they earned in America, the farmers hoped to return to Poland and buy more land.

Once a farmer decided to leave for America, he first needed money. He had to buy a boat ticket and needed extra money for food and a place to stay once he arrived in America. Most peasants earned and saved enough money for a ticket. Others had relatives in America send them a ticket. Wives and children usually stayed on the farm and continued to work the land. In some cases, farmers would give the land to their relatives.

Poor peasant farmers brought few belongings with them to America. Some farmers brought blankets to use as beds on the ship. Most brought a suitcase or bag with clothes plus a few letters from relatives already in America.

Most Polish emigrants traveled by foot, horse-drawn cart, barge, or train to the cities of Hamburg or Bremen in Germany. They waited there for a ship bound for America to arrive in port. The wait lasted a few days to several

Polish men had to line up and show their shipping documents. This paperwork let the men board the ship.

weeks. The emigrants used their savings to pay for food and a place to stay while they waited. Most Polish emigrants stayed together in boardinghouses until a ship arrived.

When a ship arrived in port, the emigrants began the journey across the Atlantic Ocean. Most emigrants could afford only the cheapest fares. They bought tickets in the ship's steerage section, the lowest, darkest part of the ship.

The trip to America took from five weeks to two months, depending on the ship's speed. Emigrants boarded sailing ships that were designed to carry cargo such as sacks of grain. Usually, the ship's crew laid boards over the cargo to create a temporary deck. Passengers had to make the best of their crowded, shabby quarters.

By the 1870s, steamships carried passengers back and forth across the Atlantic in 10 to 14 days. People who could afford to pay the first- or second-class fare had private rooms. But most Polish immigrants could only afford third-class or steerage tickets. They stayed in the lower decks furnished with hundreds of wooden bunk beds. These lower decks were as uncomfortable as those on the sailing ships, but the trip was shorter. Stormy weather sometimes made the trip across the ocean stretch to three or four weeks.

The trip across the ocean was rough for all the steerage passengers. The ship's constant rocking in the waves made many passengers seasick. Many stayed in their wooden bunk beds all day and tried to sleep. On clear days, the passengers came up on the top deck to breathe the fresh air and look out over the huge ocean. As the days passed, they looked out to sea, hoping for a view of American land.

"I would like to tell you how I have managed. I got on board ship on the 23rd and the voyage took 22 days. The weather was very bad and I had a bad trip. I arrived in America on Christmas day. That whole day I could not find my brother. So I went to some good people where I got food and a place to sleep. I wrote to my brother and he came for me."

—H. Davidson,
letter dated December 27, 1890

Polish Jewish Immigrants ★

By 1939, more than 3 million European Jews were living in Poland. Many Polish Jews lived in large cities and worked as bankers, merchants, or skilled tradespeople. Polish Jews came to America for different reasons than the poor peasant farmers.

On September 1, 1939, the German army attacked Poland from the west. This action began World War II (1939–1945). On September 17, the Soviet Union's army invaded Poland from the east. Germany's leader, Adolf Hitler, planned to rid Europe of all Jewish people. Hitler's soldiers arrested and sent Jewish people to death camps. The largest death camp was Auschwitz, located in Nazi-occupied southern Poland.

Many people were killed during the Nazi and Soviet invasions. More than 3 million Polish Jews died. About 3 million Polish Christians also died.

By the end of World War II, at least 200,000 Polish Jews survived. Some of these survivors stayed in Poland and helped rebuild their homes and neighborhoods. Many emigrated to America or Israel.

ARRIVING IN AMERICA

After many days at sea, the immigrants sailed into New York Harbor. They saw the Statue of Liberty as they sailed to a pier. The statue became a symbol for many immigrants of the opportunities in America.

Immigration officials directed people to different waiting lines as they stepped off the ship. Every immigrant had to show travel papers, but not everyone had to pass through a health inspection. Immigrants who had bought first- or second-class tickets were allowed to be on their way. Officials reasoned that people who could afford an expensive steamship ticket were probably in good health.

Most of the immigrants, including the Poles, had to wait to pass a health inspection. Poorer people could afford only third-class or steerage tickets. Officials were afraid that these people might be carrying diseases that would make other Americans sick. They also wanted to be sure that new immigrants were healthy enough to work and support themselves in America.

First, a doctor looked over each immigrant for signs of diseases. Doctors checked for rashes and coughs. When the doctors decided someone had a serious disease, they marked the immigrant's coat with chalk. Some chalk-marked immigrants went to an Ellis Island hospital to recover. Others were sent back to the port where they had started.

Many Polish wives and children were happy to arrive in America. This Polish family came to America in 1948.

Ellis Island

★

In 1892, Ellis Island opened as a station for immigration. It had 12 buildings including four hospitals, a record storage office, and a huge kitchen. The large, two-story processing building (above) was the first stop for thousands of immigrants, including Poles.

During the late 1800s and early 1900s, more than 20 million immigrants passed through Ellis Island.

Most of the Polish immigrants arrived at this time. Ellis Island closed as an immigration station in 1954.

In 1965, Ellis Island was declared part of the Statue of Liberty National Monument. After repairs and improvements, it opened to the public in 1990 as a museum. About 40 percent of all people living in the United States today have an ancestor who arrived in America at Ellis Island.

★

After the health examination, immigrants waited in other long lines. An inspector asked immigrants their names and the name of their home villages. Inspectors wrote this information in a logbook.

The wait in line took about three to five hours for healthy immigrants who had their travel documents in order. These people then took a ferryboat or barge back to the pier and entered New York City. Immigrants who did not have their necessary travel papers had to wait several days. During that time, they stayed in one of the buildings on Ellis Island.

Many Polish immigrants who came to America in the 1890s were met by relatives. These family members already had homes and jobs in the city. Those who did not have relatives in New York City boarded trains and traveled to other cities to find their relatives.

Poles who did not have family to meet them had to find shelter and work right away. Many of these immigrants had experience working only on farms. But by the 1880s, America needed factory workers more than it needed farmers. These immigrants began to work in factories in New York, Detroit, and Chicago. They operated large machines that made clothing, soap, and other products for the American people. Others labored in the coal mines in eastern states including West Virginia and Pennsylvania.

★ **Polish Names** ★

When Polish immigrants came to America, many people could not pronounce their names. Polish American children quickly began to use the Americanized version of their names.

The Polish name	in English is
Czesław	Chester/Chet
Elżbieta	Elizabeth
Ewa	Eve
Franciszek	Frank/Francis
Jan	John
Janina	Jennifer/Jenny
Jerzy	George
Józefa	Josephine
Katarzyna	Catherine/Kate
Małgorzata	Margaret
Maria	Mary
Mateusz	Matthew/Matt
Mikołaj	Nicholas
Piotr	Peter
Stanisław	Stan
Teresa	Theresa

In the late 1800s and early 1900s, Polish immigrant children found work in America's many factories. As unskilled laborers, they earned only the lowest salaries that factory owners paid to their workers.

At first, Americans were unconcerned with the Polish immigrants. Factory managers and coal mine operators needed all the labor they could find. Polish immigrants worked hard and earned the reputation of being stronger than other immigrant factory workers.

During the 1890s the attitude of many Americans began to change. Many Polish immigrants were given difficult jobs that paid very little. The immigrants began to demand their rights as American citizens. They held strikes and led marches at the factories. These protests angered the owners of the American factories. People's negative attitudes toward the Poles grew even stronger in the 1920s.

The stock market crash in 1929 greatly impacted the working life of the Polish immigrants. To make up for the money lost in the stock market crash, factory owners began to cut wages and speed up the assembly lines. Polish immigrants were some of the hardest hit by these changes. Polish immigrants continued to struggle for better working conditions. They fought for the rights of all workers.

SURVIVING IN AMERICA

Polish immigrants worked in Detroit's automobile factories, assembling cars for the growing population in America.

 bout 2 million Polish immigrants arrived in America in the late 1880s and early 1900s. American factory owners needed workers to run machines to make fabric, soap, paper, and other products. The immigrants settled in the cities to work in the factories.

Polish Americans found work in several large American cities. Men worked in the new automobile factories in Detroit, Michigan. They also found work in the slaughterhouses in Chicago. Some Polish immigrants traveled to Pennsylvania and West Virginia to work in the coal mines. Many Polish women worked in garment factories.

Some unmarried women worked as maids. A job as a maid was considered to be better than factory work. Very few Polish girls were hired as maids because they knew little English.

Polish immigrants worked hard, but their difficulty with the English language kept them from blending in with other Americans. Store clerks often made fun of the Polish women who had trouble pronouncing the items they wanted to buy. In school, students teased the Polish children because of their accents. Factory owners gave Polish men low-paying jobs because they had trouble speaking English.

Polish neighborhoods, like the Hamtramck Polonia in Detroit, included homes, shops, schools, and a church. In these close communities, people said their prayers in Polish, ate Polish food, and practiced Polish customs.

Polish immigrant families wanted to be near their churches and the factories and mines where they worked. Soon, whole neighborhoods were made up of Polish Americans. Polish communities often were called Polonia. The neighborhoods featured newspapers, theaters, radio stations, dance halls, and clubs.

Polonia neighborhoods were filled with Polish stores. Grocers sold many traditional Polish foods including Polish

dill pickles, which are made from small cucumbers. Polish butchers offered meats for bigos, a stew made with pork, chicken, and a Polish sausage called kielbasa.

Polish Catholic priests also came to the United States. They helped Polish immigrants build churches in their neighborhoods. The priests said mass using the Polish language. But some American Catholic priests thought that the mass should only be said in traditional Latin. These priests wanted to Americanize the Polish masses. The Polish priests resisted, however. They wanted to keep their Polish traditions.

The large Catholic churches were social gathering places for Polish Americans. They felt at home talking to people who were trying to find their way in a new country. Polish nuns taught students in schools built next to the churches.

By the 1860s, immigrants began establishing Polish communities in Chicago. The women and men worked in the city's garment-making shops, slaughterhouses, and

Polish women often worked in factories to help support their families. Many Polish American women found jobs in garment factories, sewing all types of clothing.

"I make six dollars and a few cents a week and I pay two dollars a week for board . . . I go to work at sewing at seven and we do piecework. We have an hour off for dinner and 6 of us work there now. Dear Mama, if I could, I would like to spend one hour with you, but nothing can be done about that. In America, I cannot just gather up money, I have to work for it. But it is, nevertheless, always easier here than it is there with you regarding money."

— Michelle Goczeszka, letter dated January 22, 1891

Polish American miners joined together to protect workers from the dangers of their job. They created unions to force mine owners to pay fair wages and make mine work safer.

steel plants. They also began to buy the homes they once had rented. By 1920, more than 400,000 Polish Americans lived in Chicago, which was more than any other single city except in Poland itself.

Living in the same neighborhoods helped many Poles adjust to life away from their home country. But living together did not stop the negative feelings others had toward Polish Americans.

Immigrants who worked in the coal mines spent long hours in the dangerous, sooty mines. In small shacks near the mines, the Polish immigrants lived with immigrants from many other countries. These homes were more run down than the peasant cottages back in Poland.

Some coal mines in America had reached depths of 1,500 feet (457 meters). Without good systems to bring fresh air into the deep mines, workers were at great risk. Sometimes methane gas from the coal would build up in the mine shaft. This gas is poisonous to breathe and often would catch fire and explode. Miners expected to be paid well for the risks of their job. But mine owners sometimes cut the wages of the miners to make bigger profits.

Despite dangerous working conditions, Polish immigrants believed they could improve their way of life. They held strikes, formed groups, and joined unions to increase wages and improve working conditions. They worked hard to become educated, middle-class Americans.

KEEPING TRADITIONS

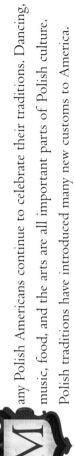

Many Polish Americans continue to celebrate their traditions. Dancing, music, food, and the arts are all important parts of Polish culture. Polish traditions have introduced many new customs to America.

Polish Americans often wear traditional clothing to celebrate in parades and on some church holidays. Each region of Poland had its own special style of dress. Almost all of these costumes included the colors red and white, which are the national colors of Poland. Women and girls wear colorful skirts and white blouses. They wear embroidered aprons over their skirts and colorful beads. Many wear flowers in their hair. Men and boys wear brightly striped pants tucked into red or black boots.

Two types of folk art that Polish Americans still enjoy are pisanki and wycinanki. Pisanki is the art of decorating eggs with melted wax and dye. The finished eggs have fancy designs in lighter colors and then are dyed a deep purple or other dark color. Wycinanki is the art of cutting paper into very fancy decorations.

Polish food includes many dishes that can be hot, sweet, or sour. The traditional main Polish meal is called obiad, which is eaten early in the afternoon. An obiad contains three courses. Soup is the first course and includes a hearty soup such as mushroom, barszcz, potato, or sour rye, or a lighter soup, such as chilled gooseberry soup. The main course is

Traditional Polish costumes include the Polish national colors of red and white.

usually a meat dish of roast pork with prunes or roast duck with apples. The last course is dessert. People enjoy many Polish desserts. Cheesecake, made with ricotta cheese, is one favorite. An apple cake called szarlotka is another tasty Polish dessert.

Today, Americans eat many of the food dishes Polish immigrants have long enjoyed. Kielbasa is smoked sausage that is one of Poland's most popular foods. Many baseball parks, fairs, and grocery stores sell kielbasa. Pierogi are dumplings stuffed with meat, cabbage, potatoes, or cheese.

Religion has continued to be an important part of Polish American life. Many Polish Americans are Roman Catholic. They celebrate traditional Christian holidays such as Easter and Christmas as well as Lent and Advent, the four-week period before Christmas.

Polish American weddings most often are solemn, religious celebrations. Some of these weddings were once celebrated for two days or more. Guests attended the wedding ceremony, ate huge meals, and danced all through the night. Today, many Polish American weddings last an entire day. Before the bride and groom leave for church, their parents bless them with holy water. At the reception, the bride and groom walk around a dining table three times for good luck.

Polish Americans celebrated the first Polish Day on October 7, 1893, to express their culture and heritage. The celebration included the first annual Polish Day parade through Chicago. Polish police officers led the parade. More than 50,000 Polish Americans marched in the parade. Crowds of hundreds of thousands watched as

Babka is a sweet, cakelike bread made with chocolate, cheese, raisins, or prunes.

The day before Lent is known as Paczki Day in some areas with large Polish populations, such as in Detroit. Lent begins the 40-day period before the Christian holiday of Easter. Many Polish people eat paczki, a fruit-filled frosted doughnut on Paczki Day.

★ Chocolate Babka ★

What You Need

Ingredients:

nonstick cooking spray

2 cups (500 mL) flour

$1/3$ cup (75 mL) unsweetened cocoa

$1\,1/2$ teaspoons (7 mL) baking powder

$3/4$ teaspoon (3 mL) baking soda

1 teaspoon (5 mL) cinnamon

$1/2$ teaspoon (2 mL) salt

1 cup (250 mL) unsalted butter, softened

$1\,1/4$ cups (300 mL) sugar

1 teaspoon (5 mL) vanilla

3 eggs

1 cup (250 mL) sour cream

1 cup (250 mL) chocolate chips

1 cup (250 mL) pecan pieces

$1/4$ cup (50 mL) sugar

1 teaspoon (5 mL) cinnamon

Equipment:

tube pan

flour sifter

measuring cups

measuring spoons

2 medium bowls

electric mixer

small bowl

knife

aluminum foil

wire rack

What You Do

1. Coat inside of tube pan with nonstick cooking spray.

2. In a medium bowl, sift together the flour, cocoa, baking powder, baking soda, cinnamon, and salt. Set aside.

3. In another medium bowl, beat the butter and sugar with the electric mixer on high speed until mixture is light and fluffy.

4. On medium speed, beat in the vanilla and the eggs, one at a time.

5. Add a little bit of the flour mixture and then a little bit of the sour cream into the butter mixture. Beat on low speed. Repeat until all the flour mixture and all the sour cream are added. Set aside.

6. Make a crumb mixture in a small bowl by combining chocolate chips, pecans, $1/4$ cup sugar, and 1 teaspoon cinnamon. Spread half of the batter in the bottom of the tube pan. Sprinkle with half of the crumb mixture. Pour in the remaining batter, and sprinkle with the remaining crumb mixture.

7. Quickly and gently cut through the batter and crumbs in an up and down motion with a knife. Lightly rap the pan once against a hard surface to settle the batter.

8. Cover the top of the cake with aluminum foil.

9. Bake at 350°F (175°C) for 45 to 60 minutes until a knife inserted halfway into the cake comes out clean.

10. Cool the cake in the pan on a wire rack for 30 minutes. Turn the cake pan upside down onto a wire rack and cool completely.

Makes 1 cake

Polish folk dancers perform traditional dances such as the mazurka at Polish festivals across the United States.

military companies, church societies, and bands marched in the first annual parade.

In 1937, Polish Americans celebrated the first Pulaski Day to honor Count Casimir Pulaski. This Polish American fought and died for America during the Revolutionary War.

America's largest Polish festival, Polish Fest, is held each summer in Milwaukee, Wisconsin. The festival includes a piano contest and plenty of Polish food, dancing, and music.

The mazurka is a Polish dance performed with fast and wild steps. Performers spin, kick, crouch, and then leap high in the air. Many people enjoy the polka, a dance set to the accordion music that Polish Americans have adopted as their own.

More than 9.3 million people in the United States today are Polish American. They are the ninth largest ethnic group in the United States.

★ Make a Family Tree ★

Genealogy is the study of family history. Genealogists often record this history in the form of a family tree. This chart records a person's ancestors, such as parents, grandparents, and great-grandparents.

Start your own family tree with the names of your parents and grandparents. Ask family members for their full names, including their middle names. Remember that your mother and grandmothers likely had a different last name before they were married. This name, called a maiden name, probably is the same as their fathers' last name.

Making a family tree helps you to know your ancestors and the countries from which they emigrated. Some people include the dates and places of birth with each name on their family tree. Knowing when and where these relatives were born will help you understand from which immigrant groups you have descended.

There are many ways to find information for your family tree. Ask for information from your parents, grandparents, and as many other older members of your family as you can. Some people research official birth and death records to find the full names of relatives. Genealogical societies often have information that will help with family tree research. If you know the cemetery where family members are buried, you may find some of the information you need on the gravestones.

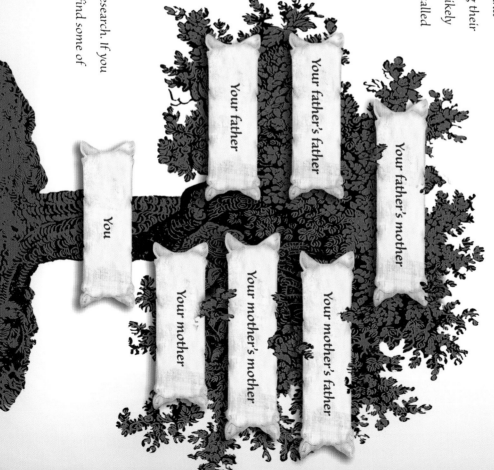

Your father

Your father's father

Your father's mother

You

Your mother

Your mother's mother

Your mother's father

★ T I M E L I N E ★

1500–1771
Nobles rule Poland, setting up a system of serfdom. Peasants work the farms in exchange for protection and land rights.

1500

1700

1772
Russia, Prussia, and Austria invade Poland. They divide a portion of Poland into Russian Poland, Prussian Poland, and Galicia.

1776
Polish American Tadeusz Kosciuszko arrives in America. He is appointed as a colonel in the American Revolutionary War.

1795
Russia, Prussia, and Austria invade Poland a third time, erasing Poland as a country.

1800

1854
The first Polish community is established in Panna Maria, Texas.

1892
Ellis Island opens. Almost 3 million Polish immigrants pass through Ellis Island over the next 30 years.

1893
Polish Americans celebrate the first Polish Day on October 7.

1900

1918
Poland regains its independence after 123 years.

1920
More than 400,000 Polish Americans are living in Chicago.

1937
Polish Americans celebrate the first Pulaski Day in New York City to honor Count Casimir Pulaski.

1986
Polish American Heritage Month becomes a national celebration in America.

★ **Pat Benatar** (1953–) Benatar was born Pat Andrzejewski in Brooklyn, New York. She became famous as a rock star in 1980 with her first album, *In the Heat of the Night*. She has won four Grammy Awards for best female rock vocal performance.

★ **Wayne Gretzky** (1961–) Gretzky was born in Brantford, Ontario, Canada. His wife and family have lived in both California and New York. In 1979, Gretzky began to play for the National Hockey League (NHL). He quickly became one of the NHL's best players. Gretzky is one of only four players in NHL history to score more than 700 goals. His nickname is "The Great One."

★ **Tadeusz Kosciuszko** (1746–1817) In 1776, Kosciuszko came to America. He was one of the first foreign volunteers to offer aid to the American Revolutionary army. Kosciuszko was appointed the rank of colonel. In 1794, he returned to Poland where he fought for Poland's independence from Russia. Kosciuszko is often called the "Hero of Two Worlds."

★ **Martha Stewart** (1941–) Stewart was born Martha Kostyra and grew up in Nutley, New Jersey. In 1972, she started her own food business. Her specialty is showing people how to use everyday materials to create fun and creative objects to decorate a home. Today, she oversees a monthly magazine, *Martha Stewart Living*, and stars in her own TV show.

★ **Stephen Wozniak** (1950–) Wozniak is an electronics engineer who helped create the personal computer industry of the 1980s. Along with Steve Jobs, Wozniak co-founded Apple Computer, Inc.

Wayne Gretzky

Martha Stewart

29

Words to Know

accent (AK-sent)—the way a person pronounces words

ancestor (AN-sess-tur)—a family member who lived a long time ago

contaminated (kuhn-TAM-uh-nay-tid)—dirty or unfit for use

culture (KUHL-chur)—a way of life, ideas, customs, and traditions of a certain group of people

emigrant (EM-uh-gruhnt)—a person who leaves his or her own country in order to live in another country

ethnic (ETH-nik)—to do with a group of people sharing the same national origins, language, or culture

foreign (FOR-uhn)—coming from another country

immigrant (IM-uh-gruhnt)—a person who comes to another country to live permanently

methane (METH-ane)—a colorless, odorless gas that burns easily

noble (NOH-buhl)—a wealthy, upper-class person of high rank

peasant (PEZ-uhnt)—someone who works on or owns a small farm, especially in Europe and in Asian nations

rebel (ri-BEL)—to fight against a government or against the people in charge of something

serfdom (SURF-duhm)—the state of being owned by a noble and treated like a slave

survive (sur-VIVE)—to stay alive through or after some dangerous event

temporary (TEM-puh-rer-ee)—lasting only for a short time

To Learn More

Armstrong, Jennifer. *Theodore Roosevelt: Letters from a Young Coal Miner.* Dear Mr. President. Delray Beach, Fla.: Winslow Press, 2000.

Bartoletti, Susan Campbell. *A Coal Miner's Bride: The Diary of Anetka Kaminska.* Dear America. New York: Scholastic, 2000.

Dolan, Sean. *The Polish Americans.* The Immigrant Experience. New York: Chelsea House Publishers, 1997.

Nickles, Greg. *The Poles.* We Came to North America. New York: Crabtree Publishing, 2001.

Raphael, Marie. *Streets of Gold: A Novel.* New York: Persea Books, 2001.

Places to Write and Visit

Chappell Hill Historical Museum
9220 Poplar Street
Chappell Hill, TX 77426

Polish American Cultural Center Museum
308 Walnut Street
Philadelphia, PA 19106-3881

Polish American Cultural Society of Metropolitan St. Louis
10257 Halls Ferry Road
St. Louis, MO 63136-4315

The Polish American Museum
16 Belleview Avenue
Port Washington, NY 11050-3607

Polish Center of Wisconsin
6941 South 68th Street
Franklin, WI 53132-8237

The Polish Museum of America
984 North Milwaukee Avenue
Chicago, IL 60622

Internet Sites

Visit the FactHound at http://www.facthound.com
FactHound offers a safe, fun way to find Internet sites related to this book.
All of the sites on FactHound have been researched by our staff.

Here's how:
1. Visit the FactHound home page.
2. Enter a search word related to this book, or type in this
   special code: **0736812083**.
3. Click on the Fetch It button.

Your trusty friend FactHound will fetch the best sites for you!

Index

Auschwitz, 13
Austria, 6, 7

Chicago, 4, 16, 18, 20–21, 22, 24

death camps, 13
Detroit, 4, 16, 18, 19, 24
disease, 14
documents, 10, 14, 16

Ellis Island, 14, 15, 16

farm, 6, 7, 8, 10, 16
folk art, 8, 9, 22

Galicia, 7, 8

nobles, 4, 6, 7

peasants, 6, 7, 8, 10, 13
Polish Jews, 13
Polonia, 19, 22, 24
Prussia, 6, 7, 8

religion, 7, 8, 13, 19, 20, 24
Russia, 6, 7, 8

school, 6, 7, 18, 19, 20
serfdom, 6, 8
ships, 5, 10, 12, 14
Statue of Liberty, 14, 15
steerage, 12, 14

traditions, 8, 20, 22–24, 26